SONGS FOR MY FATHERS

About the Author

Gary Smith was born in Cincinnati, Ohio. He earned his Bachelor of Arts degree in English at Boston University in 1972, his Master of Arts at the University of Chicago in 1974, and his Doctor of Philosophy at Stanford University in 1981.

Dr. Smith has published poems in a number of literary magazines, including *Poetry, Descant, Wascana Review, Portland Review, Impact, The American Literary Review, Dickinson Studies, Poet Lore, Occident, Sequoia, permafrost,* and *Three Sisters.*

The poet received The Clarence Urmy Award for his poetry in 1977 and The Academy of American Poets Award in 1978.

Financial support was provided by The Illinois Arts Council during the writing of *Songs for My Fathers.*

Songs for My Fathers

Poems

by

Gary Smith

Detroit
LOTUS PRESS
1984

Lotus Press, Inc.
"Flower of a New Nile"
Post Office Box 21607
Detroit, Michigan 48221

Foreword

Songs for My Fathers was written over a five year period, 1975-1980, when I lived in San Jose, California, and attended Stanford University as a graduate student in American literature. As *songs,* the poems are primarily celebratory pieces — near sonnets — that reflect the continuities within the Afro-American literary tradition. In this sense, while writing the poems, I was acutely aware of how the poetry of Phillis Wheatley, for example, speaks to the poetry of Jupiter Hammond or how the poems of George M. Horton are the pretexts for the poems of Robert E. Hayden. I have attempted to reconstruct these *speech acts*, to substantiate their historical realities and myths, and to add my own poetic voice to the dialogues.

The title, then, is hardly autobiographical, nor does it intentionally overlook the two women poets whom I address, Emily Dickinson and Gwendolyn Brooks. The ambiguities of gender and race are subordinate to the unmistakable themes to which all the poets devote their work: artistic freedom and the primacy of the poetic act.

In publishing my first volume, I wish to express a personal debt of gratitude to Naomi L. Madgett, whose Lotus Press continues to bloom while other, more endowed publishers have turned their presses into prose plants.

Finally, I dedicate this book to two extraordinary teachers: Samuel W. Allen and Terence J. Glenn.

G.S.
February, 1984

Contents

The Penitential Cries of Jupiter Hammond

(*ca.* 1711-1806)

The Penitential Cries of Jupiter Hammond
(ca. 1711-1806)

1

The Long Island sound, the pitiless clamor
of the ocean's bell
      and always, always, the sense
of loss, of imminent or apparent death;
here, the freeman, given to ideals,
sees his own reflection in the turbulence
and knows, therein, all life is flux;
a finger-size bubble momentarily spared
the sudden fate of things born to die.

But how, then, for a slave whose life
is owed to another: whose goodness
is patience ground to a hopeful dust?

What does he hear when the bell tolls
yet another lost soul to perdition —
does his tongue harden in his mouth?

Jupiter Hammond

2

Apart from the musty slave quarters,
but in earshot of the master bedroom —

A small man, compact yet portly,
his domed head fizzled with gray hair
and the line of mouth, severe and uncut,
which, when opened, shows years of toil.

Ground to a gritty resonance, your voice,
over the years had ceased to pitch forth;
but rather was swallowed inside
the cup of your lifelong bondage.

Come, Jupiter, let us pray,
I overhear your Master's command.

And you, long used to slavery's irony,
entered the room and knelt beside him.

Jupiter Hammond

3

Your poem to Phillis, hardly a poem,
born of the desire to touch another
who, like you, had heeded the Revival;
or followed the Pilgrims whose faith
was tempered by suffering — but whose
suffering was tempered by slavery.

Two caged larks, trained in song,
your bright, African plummage wilted
in the frigid New England climate;
and the sense, too, of longing blunted
by patience which holds its breath.

Yet envious, still wondrous of how
poor Phillis had managed her bondage,
you wrote to ask if her soul was saved.

Jupiter Hammond

4

My old Negroes are to be provided for,
your Master willed, the first of three
who carried you from place to place
like an overcoat bundled in the armpit.

Henry Lloyd, his son Joseph and grandson;
yet not one perceptive enough to see
the man or mask — the human being apart
from what he is taught to say or do.

That you outlived all three was not fate;
but rather the distilled vapor of faith —
the drawhorse hitched to its wagonload
that stamps its hoof-print in the snow.

But where, then, is your own grave;
who inherited the chore of burying you?

Jupiter Hammond

5

The winter of your death, I imagine
you wandering past the sea-scoured
coastline of Lloyd's Estate.
                    Utterly lost,
alone, barely able to tell where the shore
breaks free of the receding, blue horizon.

Your incessant quarrel with God over;
yet the leg-iron you wore like a mantle
still fastened you to one place, one time.

What miracles did you expect there —
the Red Sea's parting at Moses' command;
or Jonah's descent into the whale's belly?

Surely not this quiet leave-taking —
one man pitted against the ungodly,
and psalms you could vaguely recall.

Some Rumors About Phillis Wheatley

(*ca.* 1753-1784)

Some Rumors About Phillis Wheatley
(ca. 1753-1784)

1

Three years shy of your tenth birthday,
they sold you, so I'm told, as a slave
to Mistress Wheatley.
                        You were fragile-
sickly, a poor specimen whose body
had to be sponged-free of its sweat.

In the heated air of the auction room,
upon a slave block, you stood alone
in the close ranks of adolescent girls.
A wilted, black poppy whose dress
was a torn patch of dirty carpet.

What did you think then — how think! —
when the auctioneer pried your lips open
and saw the stems of unformed teeth
cut into the soft purple of your gums?

Phillis Wheatley

2

Daybreak and the unkept promise of sleep
found you spooned in the hold of a ship.

The darkness, there, clung to your body
like excrement.
                    Three weeks from Boston,
but fourteen years from the American Republic!
A prospective slave girl stolen from
                Afric's fancied happy seat.

Later, you remembered nothing of the voyage,
nothing of the dead shackled hand to foot;
or your hapless tribesmen tossed overboard
like sacraments to the waiting sharks.

Only your mother's memory surfaced again.
The humble black woman who rose early
out of lifelong habit and, from a claypot,
poured fresh water to the rising sun.

Phillis Wheatley

3

Home, then, Boston — a new name and identity —
the sleeping child bundled on the carriage,
whose every heart murmur was attended
like some prized yet endangered animal.

Master Wheatley — the tailored Puritan —
still questioned the unseemly bargain:

*What a price in gold for a slave-girl
who evidently won't last the winter?*

But Mistress Wheatley wanted insurance
against the vicissitudes of declining age —
sickness, death, and its uncertain pain:

A domestic type who'll serve me well.

Her eyes on Heaven, his on the road ahead,
and the motherless child shivering in the cold.

Phillis Wheatley

4

Slavery made you a poet — not religion!
Despite Jefferson, democracy's aristocrat,
who only saw the cloak of your race —
not his own ambivalence about slavery.

For those who still question your art,
let them count the many who neither saw
nor imagined a life apart from bondage;
who, if they lacked courage, had conviction
to smother oppression with blameless praise!

But you, Phillis, neither slave nor free,
were an enigma for Tories and Whigs alike.
You found your gift in well-placed rhymes;
a painted bird that eluded its captors
and gave mockery a cutting new name.

Phillis Wheatley

5

The one portrait that survives shows you seated
at a spherical drawing table — tilted upright
to lie about perspective! — a copybook and inkpot
juxtaposed against leaves of lined white paper;
a ruffled bonnet knotted at the top of your head,
and a corseted evening gown with traces of silk.

Our imaginary poetess in an imaginary picture!

We learn all we know from Mistress Wheatley:
I like that my Phillis be dress'd plain,

and the dishonest complacency of the age.
Your angled nose, pursed mouth, and glazed eyes.

But in the persistence of your arms, the picture
departs from the commonplace.
                              In them, it
shows how, with barbed pen, you stalked the Muse.

Phillis Wheatley

6

Crossing the Midatlantic again, this time
the esteemed poetess, the refined African
who was allowed to sit alone on ship deck;
unless the Muse spoke and you did not hear.

At one remove from Boston, the distant rumblings
of the still-unborn Republic.
>   *A fine passage*
> *of five weeks with young Master Wheatley.*

The letter of goodwill to Countess Huntingdon.

And at night, I'm told, you overheard
the human cargo groan in its manacles;
the shouts of deliverance when the seas calmed,
and buckets of water were lowered into the hold.

But, again, on ship deck — braving the Atlantic froth —
you wrote of home, your Mistress, and the glory ahead.

Phillis Wheatley

7

Always the poetess, even during the war,
when the Wheatley household — exiles at home —
moved first to Providence, later to Chelsea —
one step ahead of the embattled armies!

The angry, prosaic tenor of the times
drowned your cherubic elegies in protest.

The Republic was in the throes of labor.

And you, Phillis, eighteen years a slave,
could not have known that freedom was
no gift when unadorned with civil liberty!

Nor could you have known that death —
already a member of the Wheatley family —
had claimed you, too, as its next-of-kin.

Nevertheless, unperturbed, you wrote on.

Phillis Wheatley

8

Did you marry John Peters, or he marry you?
An articulate grocer — sometimes lawyer —
disparaged by friend and foe as shiftless:

Poor Phillis let herself down by marrying!

What did you find in him, or he find in you?

That complaisant and agreeable young man,
who took your slave name — but gave another.

And while you slept ravished your maidenhead.

Was it the need to unlace piety's knot —
to sample, once, the fruit of the ungodly?

But here, again, we know little or nothing.
The poem turns back into itself.
                                    And your life,
its refrain, is as unscored as its beginning.

You bore him three children. All died in infancy.

Phillis Wheatley

9

In what urn did you cremate your griefs,
and resurrect from their ash the flint-hard
faith addressed to everyone but yourself?

Your letters to Obour — a fellow-slave and
Newport Christian — overlook the particular,
shoeless misery you suffered, in deference
to universal pain.

In the matrix of slavery, you sang —
much like a trained sparrow! — the empty
elegies of oppression: someone else's loss,
another's unfound hope.
                                    So when death
scored your breast to release its caged heart,
what wonder to those gathered in remembrance —
that beneath the layers of pious sweetness,
a smoldering ash-pit burned in black despair.

Phillis Wheatley

10

Somewhere in a dark corner of earth,
in a grave unadorned by flower or stone,
Phillis Wheatley's body and that of her
youngest child are at rest.
                Let's presume
that a fragrant tree has taken root there —
one that would not be unworthy of the body
upon which it feeds.
                Let's imagine, too,
that children, lovers, and wisemen come
to the tree and find it unwanting in fruit.

And then let's hope that — in passing —
they remember the ground upon which they sat.

For beneath its pillow of matted grass,
beneath the subsoil of rock and decay,
a mother and her child are laid to rest.

The Fate of an Innocent Dog:

George Moses Horton

(*ca.* 1797-1883)

The Fate of an Innocent Dog

George Moses Horton
(ca. 1797-1883)

1

An innocent dog is not entirely unlike
his Master.
           Both are tied to destiny's
chain, though each claims a different fate.

No matter, here, that one is black —
                    the other white;
that one is taught to heel and beg,
while the other urges him on;
or, alas, that the imaginary chain —
                    link by link —
is circuitous reasons joined by lies.

One stands convinced of his direction;
but needs the other to pull along.

Thus, George Moses Horton, a slave
of circumstances beyond his control,
trots after his Master's command;
yet, by art, stakes his mortal claim.

31

George Moses Horton

2

I imagine you a short, coarse man,
an abrupt wit who'd seize his point
and rankle until the opposition fled.

Or generous, a talkative fruit peddler,
who'd give more than he would sell
of the plush fruit in his carriage.

Or silent, a ventriloquist's dummy,
whose hinged jaws opened and closed
over the black hole of its throat.

But never alone, never without company!

Whether with the plowhorn, that molded
your rough hands into knuckles of labor;
or with the plowblade, that cut deep
into the subsoil of the earth's skin.

George Moses Horton

3

Despite yourself, you learned to beg;
a brave, black man, humbled by birth
and a tide of misfortune which left
you gasping for breath in its wake.

You spent a lifetime vainly appealing
for freedom.
            First, as the surrogate lover
whose acrostic poems embellished white love;
then, as the willful petitioner whose letters
kept more than one abolitionist in business.

But, always, the locus point of your genius,
the honed beak of your poetic enterprise
was to be free.
            Free to come and go
without the manacles of slavery soldered
to your every word, gesture, and deed.

George Moses Horton

4

The acrostic poems you wrote to embellish
white love wore thin your own patience.

They were simple affairs, word games,
you played to exact a meal or favor
from an otherwise indifferent world.

But in them, too, I imagine the longings
you rehearsed for your supplicant patrons.

A slave by definition — but man in all else —
paid to fluff pillows and tenderize emotions,
while your own love languished in its pocket!

You suffered the humiliation of witnessing
the white love that you invented coupled
like demigods in frenzied bas-relief;
but not one whispered mention of your name.

George Moses Horton

5

By rote, you learned how to rhyme;
a reluctant cowboy whose psalms
married morning to dewstung earth.

That you could have been more,
              we now take for granted —
given slavery, your Master's whims,
and the tattered copybook you owned.

But what, now, if more is less?
And your life, instead of compromise,
had been pressed into the common herd
of gelded, shackled, and woebegone slaves —
whose life-design was the expressed need

to rise each morning, last until nightfall,
then gather for sleep in dungstrewn stalls —
where their beds were made of matted straw.

Wading Through the Flood:

Emily Dickinson

(1830-1886)

Wading Through the Flood

Emily Dickinson
(1830-1886)

1

You had no trouble unholstering your sex,
imagining yourself a boy practicing drama.
The universe then was so tightly construed
that God spoke of His wrath through birds;
His magnificence was open and unflexed —
ringed bullish to a wooden waiting post.
Once we broke free of His self-conceit,
we fled Him like proverbial thieves,
tumbling down to infamy like you told.
His image always more command than play.
Thus they quibble now about the change —
how you once could quiet a field mouse
but gnaw through the doors of eternity —
all while cleaning your garden of weeds.

Emily Dickinson

2

I cannot bear to hear lesser voices;
after talking with you they seem thin —
the right intensity is somehow overplayed.
And although they bruise my patience,
it is only you who can take my guile —
even the words sink the page I read,
leaving in its wake a rippling something
which nags my understanding to pity.
Perhaps, it is only this youth I carry
like heavy cargo to pretentious coasts —
where bargains are struck for profit.
Once out of youth's pinching grip,
I will be able to bear these others
and argue the price of my old age.

Emily Dickinson

3

Who could sustain such grace?
A friend, hearing you sing, remarked
about the sherry glass you made famous.
Surely not she who communes with things —
holding their limbs like spoiled children
she has made too precious for pain.
Surely not she who can unhinge emotions
the way others unfasten winter clothes.
But it was only after hearing you sing
that he, too, saw the fastness bloom;
so unlike the wren you wanted to be —
flitting from tree limb to tree limb.
You were never mistaken about the living —
only your eyes told you from grey stone.

Emily Dickinson

4

I like to show your poems by lottery —
the numbers, not the words, incite
my enterprise, craze my expectations
that suspend so artfully with yours.
I come to them as others would pennies —
worn thumbsmooth by countless counting,
until they spend almost without will.
Their magic always mans my patience —
I want you fixed like punctual stars,
that wink in their perpetual sleep.
Or if not you, at least some closeness,
which, too, would give me comfort.
But who could correct your being,
when you are so persistent in becoming.

Emily Dickinson

5

For too long you have haunted my purpose,
like some bird returning and returning
to the same nest abandoned each fall.
The plaintive hymns you never sung
were left to sleep in battered drawers.
Once awakened, they dispatched their voices
into the universe of contending things.
Who would have thought you so bold?
Who gather, from your meekness, strength
to dispel the gnawing demands of men?
And then to find ourselves unstrung,
confronting the same God you dismembered.
I once reverenced the chance you took —
but now I find it mere self-conceit.

Emily Dickinson

6

All womanhood is shut tight in you;
I dare to say, knowing your indifference
to the tin cans thrown at your verse.
Forced to divorce yourself from life
by the teeming circumstances of living —
not the sweating pulses we count,
you pared wisdom to its seeded core.
No children, no overweening lover,
they were all fathered by your verse
that you created without maternity.
How, then, can I undo your corset;
how take such music to bed with me?
Each poem aborts my imagination —
eyeless, their hearts sink the page.

Emily Dickinson

7

Do they breathe, you asked Higgins —
that dour, mahogany man,
from whom you requested an audience.
Not now, not now, he remembered —
thinking even then of the cause
for your straggling, lost soul —
how he would untie the maidenhead,
rend the white veil of sanctity.
But you colored his patience
and created the pensive, swearing God
who swore upon the intransigent.
This was before you unwound them both —
setting one in His kingdom come,
the other in a volume of letters.

Emily Dickinson

8

Even with the habits of middle age,
I cannot get used to the process —
how it cuts and cuts until the bone,
the mortality looks through.
I wanted you public, clearly in view —
where our eyes could meet.
But you held forth like a tormentor,
aware of my patience's end, yet firm,
perhaps convinced of the necessary whip.
None of this will ever be entirely true.
The riddled silence of your knotted hair
will never be unraveled by my hands —
the obscurity will play with me,
as your smile is mistaken for truth.

Emily Dickinson

9

I've defended you against the many
who have made a madcap of you —
citing the middle years, how feverishly
you paced the house in bridal whites,
the longing of every poem you wrote —
how easily they spill into nothing.
We like to own the poets we keep —
to mother each word like obsessions.
Your company is not easily kept —
too soon, too soon you retire to bed.
A peevish old maid worrying Puritans.
If heaven had been given to you in gold,
before singing your hymns of praise,
you would have discovered copper within.

Emily Dickinson

10

The garden you worked, they've exhumed.
They seek the straggling seeds you left —
one or two poppies and more daisies
that blossom still in convoluted vases.
Even the soil is forked and divided —
the most unimagined searches made
for the buried roots of your thought.
Oh how distressed you would have been
to see the coarse eyes which open you,
sniffing your maidenhead for signs,
so sad, too, in the same morning light
you lifted as drink to your mouth.
For therein is the mystery you left —
the confluence of earth, wind, and sun.

Robert E. Hayden:

In Memoriam

(1913-1980)

Robert E. Hayden

In Memoriam
(1913-1980)

University of Chicago, 1972

1

Unfinished errands blacken my hands
like burnt cork the minstrel's face.
The harried postman's crepe soled shoes
trample tender snails to earthworms.

And you, Hayden, accounts settled,
your thick bottomed glasses sucked
against your eyes which scuttled
across the illumined page like paramecia.

All for naught,
                          you might've said,
then turned the other cheek to show
its twin, too, stung scarlet-blue
by the leather hand of misfortune.

First your father's adopted son;
later the world's adopted poet.

51

Robert E. Hayden

2

Your shy smile belonged more to politics
than art.
             Its crease, just below your nose,
tucked under when you read/blossomed
like the cereus cactus when you spoke.

And your ringlets of hair brushed back
resembled fishhook tendrils in water.

But your eyes at work behind the pages
tenderized everything you said.
                        They floated
free of the tide/lift of your voice
like twin buoys the wave laps,
before coming to rest on the audience.

But you, too, wore the mask!
                        A quiet
man, more ancient than old, outraged
by the inevitability of human pain.

3

In the Louisiana Purchase, you could've passed
or, at least, affected a Gallic accent
and told them you'd come here by mistake.

Some French have bulbous noses/mouths!

But Napoleon sold his slaves.
He wanted a gilded, orderly Empire
to thumbspin like a toy for his children —
not nightmares of massed, unruly blacks.

Now, here, another Empire/another dream
which turns upon a few choice words:

Freedom. Democracy. In God We Trust.

But you were made for finer things —
tapered candles, stuffed reading chairs,
and Moses' eternal, everburning bush.

Robert E. Hayden

4

Cuernavaca, Mexico,
                             even there,
you found the poor wedged headlong
in the cornucopic meatstalls, alms-
beggars and churches, churches, stitched
upon the barren landscape like rich
patches of calico upon a quilt.

Could it ever have been otherwise?

The Incas and Aztecs had gods, too,
who demanded/received a virgin tithe!

And what of the pain drunk bull
massed for a second/third charge
into the painted veil of delusion?

Would its horns flinch if, in passing,
they struck the matador's heart?

Robert E. Hayden

5

Few of us survived the Middle Passage.
You knew this from slave narratives
sun-ripened, then scoriated/released
like maple sap into children's mouths.

And those who did still died
upon the bone-jarring beachhead,
when they were tossed ashore.

                              Why go on living?
You ask, this way: one hand
clenched hard upon the rostrum
and the other folded edgewise
deep inside your trouser pocket.

                              Why go on living?
When to survive only means another,
no less humiliating, form of death.

Because, maybe, we're men, maybe.

Robert E. Hayden

6

The Sixties hurt you.
                    More than you
were willing to admit, the riots/protests
spent your temper, even as you lost
what impoverished eye-sight you had.

You felt betrayed: *All protest is art!*

You felt misunderstood:
                    But all art is not protest!

So every reading you gave had its Barabas
who was spared the ignobility of the Cross.

Though the Seventies were better, then too,
you had detractors, impatient with craft,
who shouted down your art as appeasement.

And backstage, after yet another trial,
your face was rinsed of emotion and color —
you had to be helped to the waiting car.

Robert E. Hayden

7

Admittedly, the poems were few.
                              Nothing like
Dickinson's hard routine/Whitman's beatitude.
We live a life where a poet's measure is
the breadth of his overcoat — not the fit.

You belonged to the first row of minor poets;
the neglected ones muscled on the bookshelves,
outsung by popular culture.
                              Yet from your throat
issued the sorrow-hammered truths of a generation.

Long after the earth has been wasted;
heaven shorn of its inherent mysteries —

long after the thunderous enterprise of progress
has worn down its wheel,
                              your voice,
with others, will fill the void of what
was/could have been and is forever lost.

Robert E. Hayden

8

No marvel in this:
                    You were a poet;
nor injustice in this:
                    You were black.
For a man takes his own measure
and images his God thereafter.

Only the fearful mimic what they're not:
a crow/the eagle's hungry cry;
a hyena/the lion's lusty bite.

Only the fanciful fear the unknown
and cringe at the loss of their souls.

For as Tubman knew — lead not follow —
the moon-star that lights the way.

For as Tubman said:
                    If one fails,
cut his legs from beneath him!

Let our God, if he is just, serve us.

Robert E. Hayden

9

An adolescent, the boy you never forsook
whose thornstruck hand bloodied the page.
Sundays, too, you tiptoed away from
        the chronic angers of that house,
and found peace/solace in the nearby woods —
where you saw the spider's coffin-web.

Later, still, you found sorrow blossoms
whose heady nectar towed your heart under.

You stumbled from the garden, back to the house,
too drunk to stand against the whipping stick.

But you never forsook the boy. He lived
to write the hard truths you had learned.

And when, finally, the seeds of hate were sown,
and city after city was looted of its harvest,
you stood fast and swore your kingdom had come.

Robert E. Hayden

10

Three years short of three-score ten,
your hair clipped and a Hamletlike
tunic fastened at your throat.
                              Youth's
extravagance gone and middle age in abeyance.
Still, I imagine, you rose early out of habit —
your heart's mill grinding the minutes to pulp.

The spirit-house, your body, no longer
bending to the flowers you kept close.

And, always, your Achilles-eyes fixed
upon the fateful moment of blindness.

What terror you must have known —
a cornered beast sensing its doom,
the fall/swoop of the hawk's buckled wings,
then the bone-crushing weight of sleep.

Robert E. Hayden

11

Where are the poems of old age,
the sun soured lyrics of Mad Lear
or Macbeth's cauldron of witches?

Was there never a virgin woman
who touched you, then left you
quivering in nightsweat?
                         And, later,
returned to nurse you back to health?

Where are the giddy prophecies
of Yeats' gyre, Auden's austerity?

*A poet's business is life: either
that he lives or that he remembers.*

And what of the wild, heart longings
which flail him to sleep at night?

Those are the dreams he leaves behind.

Robert E. Hayden

12

There were moments of translucent harmony —
                                                    so rare —
your soul started ticking its watch.
What did you see then?
                                        The lynchmen
bunched around the spectacle of a hangedman —
his body frying in its own residue of fat;
or starlings awakened from evening slumber
by the sound of gunshot and the hundreds
who lay dead in the morning-after.
                                                    What
did you see and why? A perfect harmony
divorced of its masthead — grief?
                                            I see
you there, the hangedman, one starling,
your cornered eyes pressed close to the mob —
death's jurymen,
                            and your watch/soul set
to the fateful hour of deliverance.

Robert E. Hayden

13

To love a poet but not the man,
the Negro but not his mask!

We want things obviously simple —
not the pathological-laced verse
you wrote of life lived on the fringe.

Of poverty, so ancient, it no longer
remembers its proffered name.
Of love, so insensate, it no longer
bears its young.

If we cannot have our inventions,
then we destroy what is there.

Every loss diminished you!
                    And what
unforeseen horrors you could not name,
you counted, too, among the living.

Robert E. Hayden

14

Teaching was never your suit!
                  A waterless
thing, sandlocked, you were awkward
and spread-eagled before the assembly.
Their forthright manner was unsettling.
Their sharp smiles and fingers poked
through the poet to touch the man.

And you bled, there, helplessly
rolled to and fro by the jeering surf.
And not one who knew/understood enough
to break rank and unsmother you.

It was a heart-rending sight,
                     I am told.
Could I have been there to ease the pain,
find your misplaced glasses on the floor!
Or, even, to point you seaward again.

Robert E. Hayden

15

Even in death, you could not rid
yourself of the albatross, Ham's curse,
and the odor of race that shackled
your every word.
                    You wanted to see/feel
life's manifoliate bouquet,
                    the bunchy smother
of things bright green and howling red;
the ooze of sweetgum and sting of persimmon.

But, always, to be different meant
to be Negro — colorblind and woebegone —
massed in protest or lively in music!

And when, finally, after years of effort,
your diseased heart beat was silenced,
they carved your epithet in two:

A man and poet who wrote of color.

Bronzeville Lady with Hat:

Gwendolyn Brooks

(1917-   )

Bronzeville Lady with a Hat

Gwendolyn Brooks
(1917-   )

1

The wrought-iron fence is still there:
its metal braces blackened and sunbuffed
after sixty years of sedentary duty.
So too is the gate that swung carefree;
but now, at touch, bends its frame inward
in a silent, worldwise sigh of relief —
accustomed to time, the changeless changes
of the seasons and vague ideas of aristocracy.

And you, Brooks, its only caretaker,
the adolescent girl who planted petunias
around its base-roots that it might grow:
friendless, sheltered by the sun's bubble,
the daughter your mother, Keziah, crafted
like the artful words of a homespun ballad.

Gwendolyn Brooks

2

You watched your father struggle with sleep,
his workday clothes piled beside his bed,
his swollen hands buried beneath his pillow.

David, a strong man, quiet/unassuming —
he smothered his dreams so yours might live.

On those evenings when he returned home from work
with his daily catch of songs, rhymes and candy,
you were beside yourself with adolescent joy.

It was only later he became the sculptured door,
the trespass that was forbidden you.
                              The man
you could not unearth from the soil of his life.

He stood apart from life's baffling conundrums —
round, whole, completely self-contained.
                              The man
whose simple want was for a good night's sleep.

Gwendolyn Brooks

3

Lady Dunbar!
          You were christened
with the Negro poet's laurel. His
twisted smile chalked upon your face,
and the heavy/hollow scepter thrust
between your small cupped hands —
a replica of the mocked-poet's glory.

Nearkin surrounded you like marigolds —
their black faces and broad-tooth smiles
shone bright beside your imaginary fame.

Lady Dunbar!
          You stood before them
rehearsing the minced words of success;
unaware of the Negro poet's dread —
the hours he spent apart from his fame
wiping grease/burnt cork from his face.

Gwendolyn Brooks

4

Daughter of Dusk! Solomon's sun-kissed bride!
You belonged to Ham's tribe — servant of servants —
driven out of Noah's tent/exiled to Canaan.

Outside the schoolyard gate, you waited for Mabbie,
your chocolate companion — sunblotted and boisterous —
your lips pursed with longing/wanton expectation.

How could you have known she too was friendless:
a victim of the world's drunkenness, a shoeless child,
unnumbered/unwanted by those she most resembled?

How could you have known there were other Mabbies
no less misguided, no less mistaken in their identities —
persecuted in and out of their race/exiled to Canaan,
cursed for the very sin that made them human?

How could you have known Mabbie was Mabbie-to-be!

Gwendolyn Brooks

5

McKay and Cullen befriended you. *New Negroes:*
poets from the Harlem Renaissance, word-intoxicated
men apart from their race. They sought the universal
but found only the particular.
                           They wanted poetry
to be unencumbered by race/something indifferent
to the soil of time and place: hothouse blossoms
that yield their rich fragrance in cups of water.

And you, Brooks, their hopeful vessel,
the unsifted poetess who read their poems
like the word-coated leaves of the Bible,
who saw their wisdom/folly, their wheat/chaff.

But you built your kingdom, *Bronzeville*, upon
the lives of the poor, desperate and heartsick —
tenants who asked more of life than they gave.

Gwendolyn Brooks

6

When the Pulitzers called you/you were
without houselights — months behind in rent —
your kitchen boiled with friendly mice
that you did not have the heart to kill.

You danced merrily inside the darkness —
a confirmed poet, a bejewelled ring
tossed to every passerby who overheard
the gathered throng of well-wishers.

Our first Negro Laureate. . . . Our very first!

And later, when the lights were turned on,
when you had marshalled the strength to feed
those who still lingered as an afterthought,
no one knew your life would remain the same —
the congenial mice and well-rhymed poverty.

Gwendolyn Brooks

7

Chocolate Mabbie, Moe Belle, Pearl May, Annie Allen
Maud Martha, Jessie Mitchell, Hattie Scott, Old Mary

Your legion of women, battle-scarred banners of faith,
victims twice over: black/identified and woman/identified;
nameless even when their names are as common as dandelions
wedged between the hardened concrete slabs of sidewalk,
where old men and dogs gather to recount their scores.

In what sense are they contained by their lives?

Black women who huddle inside your poetic truths,
who assemble like spent/netted fish in church pews,
who return home Sundays to their men-ravaged lives.

In what sense do they contain their lives?

Each one both daughter and mother — acorn and oak —
the vessel and the water that pours from it.

Gwendolyn Brooks

8

The death of one mouse diminished you!
Its funnel-shaped head and flagellate tail
were no less divine than the human hand
that springs the iron-jaw of the trap.

Does one determine the other's fate?
                Or are they worlds apart —
your apocryphal city, *Bronzeville*, and Chicago?

One spawned in the dark rafters of poverty —
the poor, to-be-pitied children of the poor,
whose dreams ripen like yesterday's garbage.

The other secure in its whiteness/its sanctity,
the feast it makes of its merciless history:

Hog-Butcher, Politician, Ganglord and Stockbroker.

But you, Brooks, blessed/gave life to the dead mouse;
you saw the poor as people apart from their poverty.

Gwendolyn Brooks

9

Langston Hughes was your poet-idol:
the man-god whose shoes you unlaced —
the legendary poet whose lifeblood was
crushed from the paint of Negrolife.

Those evenings when you sat together,
a dinner of turkey tails shared between,
you could hardly stir the rice in its pot!

                    And Hughes,
his face coppered by cigarette smoke,
his mannish cheeks pinched with youth
and his brown eyes freckled with age.
You knew, even then, that memory is precious;
that it is bestowed to those who have lived.

And its measure is not the clamor of kings,
but the quiet work of giving: one to another.

Gwendolyn Brooks

10

The Sixties caught you napping,
a queen bee dusted with praise,
gently courted by a hive of critics.

So when the world turned/shrugged
and gave birth to poets who cried
that art was another political game —
as deadly as molotov cocktails/bullets,
you burst the chrysalis of your wings
and became a born again poet.

                                   Brightly
turbaned and gaily painted jet-black,
the scourge of art-sakists and liberals.

You became the gentlewoman whose face
mirrored the history of black Chicago —
the honey-crowned symbol of a generation.